# Keys to Meaningful Life

Rahul Singh

Copyright © 2015 Rahul Singh.

All Rights Reserved.

Cover Design : James, GoOnWrite

First Edition : July, 2015

To Baba,
who taught me how to live a meaningful life

# Introduction

How to live a meaningful life?

That's the question I asked myself more than seven years ago. And it has led to this book you are reading right now.

As the title of this book says, you will find several practical tips here which you can start to apply as soon as you read them. And soon you will be on your way to live a happy and meaningful life.

This book is organized into 35 key chapters. Each chapter is a small key towards living a more meaningful life. The more keys you implement, the more closer you will come to understand the meaning of your life.

The most basic tips are covered first, and as you move ahead, the content will become more and more advanced.

At times, some advice may seem to contradict other ones. When this happens, try to understand the context in which it's being said. Sometimes, there are more than one ways to solve a problem. Knowing both the ways can help you choose the one that suits you most.

You'll also find that some tips appear several times across different chapters in this book. This will help you to understand their importance, and the role they play in living a meaningful life.

To get the maximum benefit from this book, read a few chapters every day. Don't try to finish this book in one sitting, like a novel. This book is a result of over two and half years of meditation, and if you understand it properly, it can change your life for the better.

When you come across any thought that challenges your earlier assumptions about life, spend few minutes thinking about it. Don't accept anything blindly, but meditate and decide for yourself if what's said is true or not.

I have taken care to make this book as perfect as possible. If you still find any mistakes, do let me know and I will be happy to correct them in future updates.

So without wasting any time, let's start our journey towards a meaningful life. Find a quiet place, read slowly, and allow the words to sync within you. Everything in this book is meant exclusively for you.

Keys to Meaningful Life

# Slow Down

If your life seems busy and chaotic, just take a breathe and slow down.

If there are too many things running in your mind right now, slow down and pause for a while.

Life doesn't need to be a mental frustration. Slow down, and let life come back to its natural state, and then rest in this state of calmness and enjoy the peace that comes with it.

Too many gadgets, too much technology, create clutter in our mind and affect our mental well-being. Instead of making our life simple, they further complicate it, and make us addicted and a slave to them.

Let's slow down for a while, and instead of spending time with technology, spend some time with the beautiful gifts of Nature, which are present everywhere around us.

Take time to breathe slowly. Take time to smell a flower. Take time to walk slowly in a garden. Take time to lie down and stare at the open sky at night.

Drink a cup of tea sip by sip, read a book without any hurry, spend time with your family and have a few laughs, or listen to your grandfather's thoughts about life. This is what makes life beautiful.

Play with kids. Tell them stories of hope, faith and inspiration. Let their minds wander and imagine the magical world of fairies and gypsies.

Slow down, and fill your life with all such beautiful moments.

The world won't end if you don't check facebook or twitter for a day. It won't end if you switch of your phone and other gadgets for a day. It will still be the same.

But yes, it will be a better world for a day, because there will be one more happy and peaceful person in this world that day. And that person will be You.

Let's make an honest effort to use technology wisely and with responsibility.

Slowing down, you will come in touch with yourself. You will see your unique thoughts and the goals you had completely forgotten, once again.

You will become that kid again who always lived in the present moment; who fought with his friends one moment, and started playing with them another moment; a kid who was free from any kind of ego, who just wanted to have a good time every day.

Slow down and start doing one thing at a time. When doing work, just work. When playing games, just play. When chatting with friends, just chat. When listening to someone, just listen.

It takes time to learn something completely. It takes time to build something great. It takes time to understand yourself. It takes time to become a better person.

If you really want to live a more meaningful life, first slow down.

# Simplify Your Tech Life

Do you end up spending more time with technology gadgets than you actually want to? Do you always think as the day ends, that you should have done more work? Do you feel that you are not as productive as you really want to be?

Then, perhaps it's time for you to do some self-examination, find whether you are using technology in an optimal way, and most importantly to simplify your tech life.

The reality is, every day, we spend many hours using some form of technology. We use technology in different forms and shapes such as computers, laptops, tablets, or phones.

We spend this time using technology because

a) our work requires us to do so,

b) we want to stay socially connected,

c) we want to learn new things online, or

d) we just want to kill some time.

Whatever the reason, the reality is, we end up wasting a good part of our life consuming unwanted information via these computers and gadgets.

If you really want to make the best use of your time, you must simplify how you use technology in your everyday life.

Here are some simple steps that will help you to do so:

**Observe your daily tech usage**

Just make a note of how you spend your time with technology, in your day-to-day life. To do this, observe for one day how much time you spend in using technology and what are your daily activities. Observe it from the time you get up at morning to the time you go to sleep at night.

Don't try to think about solutions while making these observations. Be totally honest with yourself. Don't try to cheat yourself by acting differently that day. Simply observe. That's it.

**Kill those time-wasters permanently**

After observing your routine, identify what can be simplified. Watch out specially for the time-wasters.

What exactly are time-wasters? Time-wasters are those activities that don't help you grow in any way; activities that won't improve the quality of your life, personally or professionally. If possible try to eliminate them completely. Some examples of this are watching youtube videos, surfing internet aimlessly, spending too much time on facebook, twitter, whatsapp, and similar sites.

**Minimize your social media usage**

Social networking is useful, but if you get addicted to it, you can end up wasting a full day quite easily. Ask yourself if you really need to follow hundreds of people on twitter and facebook, and especially those people who haven't changed your life in any way. People who you might not even see again in real life. You don't have to follow them.

Try to reduce your following list to only relevant people on twitter and facebook. Unfollow those who just add noise and don't matter to you. Also, ask yourself if your really need to read every tweet and facebook update daily? The answer is you don't. So, don't worry if you miss anything.

**Stop being available 24×7**

It's not just following fewer people on social media. You must limit how many times you check these accounts every day. Stop automatic notifications from all applications. You don't even need to check your email every few minutes.

Stick to a fixed scheduled time. For most people once or twice a day should be sufficient, and that too if your job really requires you to do so.

**Take regular breaks at work**

Even if you reduce your tech usage, you may need to sit for long hours at your desk to do your work. So make sure that you take regular breaks at work. Small breaks help you unwind and are good for your health.

In this break-time, you can read an actual book, go for a small walk, or do some stretches to refresh your body and mind. You can also close your eyes and meditate for few minutes. A quiet and clear mind always boosts your productivity.

**Spend some quiet time away from these gadgets**

Taking breaks is a good way to refresh the mind and body. But you can only take a limited number of breaks while doing your work. That's why it is really important to spend some time completely away from all tech gadgets.

Spend at least a few hours every day without using any form of technology. Go for a long walk, meditate, or spend some quality time with your family. Make sure your phone is on silent mode and away from you. Just enjoy this time doing what you love to do, as long as it doesn't require you to stare at any kind of screen.

The true purpose of technology is to serve us and improve the quality of our life. By simplifying how we use technology, we can live a more stress-free, productive and peaceful life. So, don't wait. Start simplifying your tech life today.

# Do One Thing at a Time

When we see everyone around us multitasking, we think that it is the right way to accomplish more in less time. People who do more than one task at the same time, seem smarter and more talented than those who only do one thing at a time.

The truth is, multitasking actually results in lower productivity and poor performance. To get the best out of yourself, you should rather concentrate on doing only one task at a time.

There are many good reasons to do so.

**You will finish your work in less time.** This is because when we concentrate only on one task, we are likely to make less mistakes. Our efficiency also improves, as the only thing in our mind right then is that single activity. So naturally, we get more ideas related to our work, and we end up doing more work in less time.

**You will start excelling at your work.** When you work on one thing with deep concentration you understand it more clearly, and slowly you start getting better at it. With time, you will find that you have actually become better than most people who only do their work half-heartedly.

**You will enjoy doing your work even more.** When we start excelling in doing our work, we actually start enjoying it. The more we enjoy it, the more we want to work.

**The quality of your work will improve.** When you really enjoy doing your work and do it with excellence, then the quality of your work naturally improves.

**You will feel less worry and stress.** A great advantage of doing one thing at a time is you don't get time to worry about unnecessary stuff. As you are fully focused on doing only one thing, you don't spend any time worrying about the past or future.

**You will become more productive.** What happens when you enjoy doing your work, start excelling at it and doing it in less time? The result is you actually become more productive at doing your work.

So now when you know all the benefits of doing one thing at a time, you might as well want to know how to do this. Here is what I suggest:

First, **remove all distractions around you.** Remove all those unnecessary things that just take up space on your desk, and stick only with the most important things. Remove all unnecessary programs from your computer. Switch to full screen mode when doing your work, so that you can only see the work area on your computer.

Second, **divide your tasks in small chunks.** If you have to do a hundred things in a day, break them down into small chunks in such a way that every chunk means doing only one task; nothing more than that.

Third, **do only one chunk at a time.** Now start by doing only one small piece of work at a time. When reading something, just read. When writing, just write. Move to another chunk only when you are finished with the current one.

Finally, **focus on what you do.** Do every little task with complete focus. If any distracting thought comes to your mind, just ignore it and continue doing your work with focus.

That's it. Follow these simple steps and start doing one thing at a time. Soon, you will discover the joy of working in the present moment and will be able to manage your work life more efficiently.

# Just Be Yourself

If I had to tell you only one thing that can improve your life today, right now, it would be this : Just be yourself.

You know why? Because you only invite stress and unhappiness in your life when you try to live like someone else, or when you try to become like someone else.

It's a good thing when you see someone living a better life than yours, and if that motivates you to work hard and change your own life.

But the problem comes when you try to act and live like someone else all the time.

When you want to act, live, or work like some other successful person you're creating the circumstances that are bound to make you unhappy in future.

To live a simple, happy, and meaningful life learn to just be yourself.

When you follow your true nature you're free to do what you think is right to do. And when you do the right thing every time, you'll never regret it as long as it completely confirms with your convictions.

When you try to be someone else, that only means that you are not happy with who you are, and that's the main problem you should be worried about.

Try to become yourself first, and you'll see that people like and respect the ones who are original in what they do; others are easily forgotten as copycats.

When you live every moment of your life with who you really are, there are less desires, less unhappiness, less stress, and more of you in whatever you do.

When you act as per your inner nature, your work reflects you in itself. Your work is original, and a truer representation of your thoughts and ideas.

But when you cloud yourself with someone else's way of thinking and acting, you make decisions that you think the other person might have made in your situation.

And when you do that, you stop being yourself and start becoming more of the other person. When you do any actions based on what someone else would do, you are lying to yourself and not following your intuition.

If you keep doing this for long enough, you start to feel unhappy with yourself. You start to wonder why you aren't as appreciated or as respected as the other person whom you are trying to copy.

The reason is, you do not know what struggles and events that other person went through in his life. Every action that he did was responsible for the person he is today.

And you have your own experiences and your own decisions that you made throughout your life. And that's why you are the person you are today.

Your actions and experiences were different from the other person. So how can different actions and experiences produce the same results. They can't.

The main reason that we want to imitate someone else's life is because we think they are happier, cooler, or more successful than us.

We see the positive side of their life, which is a good thing, but we fail to see their real life and their day-to-day struggles that they go through, or have gone through, to become what they are today.

We only see the incomplete picture of their life and we think they are much better than us in such and such ways. If you only look closer and try to see their everyday life, you'll find that their life is really not as awesome as you thought it would be.

They may not have the same problems as you, but they might have another set of problems which could be even worse than yours.

The problems that you have are only yours and only you can solve them. And you can only solve them if you try to solve them in a way that's true with yourself. You cannot solve them simply by imitating someone else, and by trying to solve the problem the way they did.

To live a meaningful life you have to start first by respecting your own thoughts and intuition. If you just reflect enough on your actions everyday and keep learning from them, you'll start becoming more and more of yourself.

And your actions will start getting more and more in sync with your inner self.

And an indirect result of this is that you will start feeling happier about who you are and what you do, and will stop imitating or comparing yourself with someone else.

Everyone of us here has a similar mind and body. So don't worry about the minor differences between you and someone else. You are already perfect in everything. You just have to realize this perfectness inside you before you can start living it.

And you can start to do that today, at this moment itself, by just being yourself.

Stop comparing yourself with others. Stop imitating someone's lifestyle. Stop thinking that others are happier or better than you. Stop thinking that you are better than someone else.

Just be yourself.

Just do what you think is right to do. Just learn from your own life's experiences. Just try to work on your own thoughts, and reflect upon them every day.

And when you start living your life the way you are meant to, pass on your experiences and help others to do the same.

# Embrace Simplicity in Life

With each passing day our life seems to get more and more complicated.

Most of our complications in life come from wanting too many things in too little time.

But there is no need to complicate your life.

There are only so many things you can do in a single day. You can only push yourself to a certain limit every day.

So don't hurry. Do what you can do today, and leave the rest for tomorrow.

Every thing suffers when you do them in a hurry - your quality of work, your relationships, your inner peace. Every thing.

See the beauty of this moment. See the beauty of simplicity.

Just enjoy what you have and be happy and satisfied with it.

There is nothing to be chased, no goals to be attained, no targets to be met.

Let your worries fade away. Let your desires go

away. Let everything around you become peaceful.

Stop chasing perfection and learn to love the imperfect.

Just walk around, observe, and see how beautiful every thing already is.

When you rid yourself of every unwanted thing in your life, what remains are the simple things that are enough to live a joyful life.

Embrace this simplicity and remove the clutter from your life.

There are too many unwanted things in your life. There are too many unwanted thoughts in your mind. There are too many unwanted feelings in your heart.

You don't need them. They don't do you any good.

Let them go and be glad that they are gone.

Learn to live with less. Learn to live with the important, and discard the unimportant. Learn to see the essential from the extravagant. Learn to separate the truth from the false.

Embrace simplicity in every thing you do – from the way you work, to the way you buy things, to the way you think.

When you reduce the number of things you have to deal with every day, you reduce few other things too – you reduce stress, you reduce clutter, you reduce complexity, you reduce anxiety, you reduce greed.

The only things you increase are your peace of mind,

your happiness, your self-control.

There is power in simplicity. There is beauty in simplicity. There is joy in simplicity. And once you start to live a simple life, you'll see that there is abundance in simplicity.

Wake up to simplicity every morning. Go to sleep with simplicity every night.

To make it simple, do one thing at a time.

To make it simple, focus on one thought at a time.

To make it simple, live one moment at a time.

Life is meant to be simple and beautiful, so why are you complicating it?

# Stop Rushing Through Your Day

From the moment we get up to the moment we go to sleep, we keep rushing through our day.

We live our life as if it's a race that we need to finish in one day.

If it was only about a day, then it won't be an issue. But it's never about a single day. We keep living the same life day after day after day.

But do you ever take a pause from your daily routine and ask yourself why you keep rushing through your day.

Is this how you want to live your full life?

Probably not.

None of us want to live a hectic life.

We don't want our life to be a never-ending chase. We want it to be a happy and peaceful journey, of which we have lived every moment to its fullest.

So if we all want peace and happiness in our life, then how do we end up spending our day in chaos, running continuously from one thing to another?

The answer lies in the nature of our mind.

From morning to night, our mind keeps wandering from one thought to another without taking a break. It doesn't like to stay quiet and do nothing.

That's why, when you try to focus on one task it tells you to focus on ten different ones. Your mind, if left uncontrolled, can ruin your full day.

Thanks to our mind, we are never at peace with ourself.

We finish one task, only to run after another task.

We always look forward to the next thing to do, but we fail to give our hundred percent to what we are doing right now.

We worry how will we finish so many things in a single day. And worrying about this, we spend our full day in anxiety and tension.

Won't it be better if we could just focus our mind, and all our energy, on the present activity, and leave the other stuff for when the time comes to handle them.

So your present time is only for your present activity and your future time will be only for your future one.

This way, you don't need to create clutter in your mind, worrying about all your activities at once.

Instead, think of it as dividing your day into multiple small activities, where your mind is concerned with only one activity at any given time.

You don't need to worry about how you will get all

the remaining work done. Instead you can just focus completely on the present task, and give it your best shot.

And once you finish your present task, move on to your next task and again give it your best shot. Keep doing all your activities this way, by remaining completely immersed in the current activity.

This way, the quality of your work improves, and you feel relaxed and peaceful even if you had to do a lot of tasks in the day.

But it's not always right to blame our mind for making us rush through our day.

Sometimes, it's our own habits that cause us to do that.

We form several bad habits that keep us busy, even if we do not need to. There are so many things in our life that only add noise to our life, and which we can easily give up.

Just by reducing the time we spend online everyday, we can create enough time to do all our work without rushing through them.

If you just spent less time on twitter, facebook, and using your smartphones and tablets, then perhaps you could easily manage your day.

To break such habits which only waste our time, we have to learn to be mindful of ourself throughout the day.

By being more aware of the present moment, we can break such habits that are stopping us from living our life to the fullest.

Life becomes more joyful when you don't have to run after it.

Simply staying mindful of your every moment, might just be the thing you need to bring peace in your everyday life.

Learn to do that, and you will sail through easily even on a busy day.

# Stop Chasing the Wrong Things in Life

I know you have your personal goals in life. And you also have some unfulfilled desires in your heart that you want to fulfill some day.

But do you ever ask yourself, while pursuing your goals and running after your desires, if it's worth the time you spend thinking and acting upon them?

Many times, we chase our goals and desires in life, only to discover later that we were chasing the wrong things all the time.

Don't let this happen to you.

Assume that you already had all the things you desire for, and you met all your goals in life. What then? Would your mind be peaceful? Or would it start to form new desires and goals again?

We often think that to live a happy life we need more money, more free time, more fame, a bigger house, the latest electronic gadgets, and other luxury items. When what we really need is a peaceful mind and a contented heart to go with it.

We move from one goal to another, and we chase one

desire after another, only to find that we are still unhappy and discontent with ourself.

Do you know why this happens?

Because you chase the wrong things in life.

Instead of making your mind peaceful, you make it more and more chaotic by consuming one thing after another. Instead of making your heart content, you keep entertaining it by following one desire after another. If you want peace inside you, all this needs to stop.

Instead of chasing the wrong things, what if you chase the right ones. How different will be your life then.

Think about your daily routine and see if what you do on a day-to-day basis is worth doing in the long run. Can you replace any activity with a more meaningful one? If so, then why not replace it now.

Observe all the activities you typically do in a day. Do you find any activity that doesn't contribute to your long-term happiness and well-being, and exists only to fulfill your daily desires. Replace that, too.

Think deeply upon what you wish to achieve ultimately in your life. Is it peace, happiness, satisfaction, and the right understanding about life, or is it chaos, sadness, discontent, and ignorance about life?

The answer is obvious. We all seek permanent happiness, permanent peace, and permanent contentment in life. And that is what we should work after in our life, and not any misleading goals or any temporary pleasures and fantasies.

From time to time, you should evaluate your goals and desires. Else, if you let your desires and goals control you, you will end up wasting years and decades of your life in pursuing things that weren't worth pursuing at all right from the start.

The only worse thing than not achieving your goals, is to achieve the wrong goals.

Take some time today from your schedule, and think about it.

We already have limited time on this planet. Don't limit it further by chasing any unwanted things in life.

# Live with Less

Why live with less?

Less. Because less is simple to manage and easy to live with.

Less. Because it helps you get rid of distractions.

Less. Because it means less things to worry about.

Less. Because it helps you get rid of unwanted things in life.

Less. Because it means less clutter and more space for you to grow.

\*

Less. Because your mind and body can only do a limited things in a day.

Less. Because it helps you find focus and dedicate yourself to few things only.

\*

Less. Because it gives you enough to survive.

Less. Because it gives you enough to live a happy life.

\*

Less. Because more doesn't mean better.

Less. Because it makes you go for quality instead of quantity.

Less. Because less gives deeper and enriching experience.

*

Less. Because your time is limited.

Less. Because your time is too precious to throw away in pursuit of more.

Less. Because it gives you more time every day to grow yourself.

Less. Because it gives you more time to learn, to meditate, to sleep, and to take care of your family.

*

Less. Because it makes you shift your focus from money to other important things in life.

Less. Because it helps you separate the important from the unimportant.

Less. Because it makes you realize your basic needs, and makes you respect the basic needs of others.

Less. Because it makes you realize how similar you are to others, and that differences exist only in the mind.

*

Less. Because it makes you happily share with others.

Less. Because it makes you kind and compassionate.

Less. Because it's the only way to have peace in your life.

\*

Less. Because it makes you live in the now, instead of the past or future.

Less. Because that's the path ancient sages and yogis took to figure out the meaning of life.

Less. Because it makes you stop looking outside, and start looking within.

Less. Because it gives you time to discover yourself.

Less. Because it brings you to the reality of life.

Less. Because it brings you close to your true nature.

Less. Because it helps you live to a higher purpose.

\*

Less. Because the desire for more never ends.

Less. Because you can't take anything with you when you leave from here.

Less. Because that's the only way we can live in harmony and peace together.

Less. Because there isn't enough in the world to satisfy everyone's desires.

Less. Because we all can have it without fighting each other.

Less. Because the planet can no longer afford to give all of us more.

Less. Because its not an option anymore, but essential for the planet to survive.

*

# Reply Selfishness with Kindness

What do you do when you come across selfish and mean people in your life?

Argue with them? Hate them? Fear them? Or wish something bad happens to them?

I don't know about you, but, earlier, when someone was selfish to me, it hurt me, and I wished someone hurt them too for what they did to me. I thought they deserved as much pain and suffering as they gave to me.

But soon I started to notice a change in me. Whenever I acted selfishly against others who were selfish to me, instead of feeling good, I felt bad from inside. I felt unhappy about my own selfishness. I saw that, in my act of replying selfishness with selfishness, I was becoming selfish in other areas of my life too.

I realized that you can't be selfish to only one person. Once you let selfishness take hold over you, you act selfishly to everyone else in your life too.

It was then that I decided that I will just follow my real nature, which was to be kind and compassionate to others. I started to reply selfishness with kindness and this made me feel good from within.

Though I wasn't emotionally strong enough then, and at times I still reacted selfishly, but slowly, slowly, I started moving from selfishness to kindness. And then I came across several moments in my life which proved to me that by being kind I was actually helping the selfish person realize his selfishness, which I couldn't do before by reacting selfishly to them.

And now, when I no longer give away to such feelings I feel peace inside me, and that allows me to forgive others for their selfish acts.

And you know what, you feel much better when you forgive others for what they did to you, than when you continue to hold a grudge against them.

When others are mean to us, we try to attack back, but when we do so we unconsciously let our ego take full control over us. And then we end up doing things which we regret later.

Your ego makes you think everything in terms of 'I' and 'Me'. You think thoughts such as: I am unhappy, I am angry, He did this to me, He called me by that name.

All such things which we think in terms of 'I' or 'Me', makes us believe that we are separate from others and that our happiness is separate from others, too. This belief makes us think that we need to take control of our own happiness, and it makes us act selfishly all the time.

Instead of reacting selfishly to anyone, if you realize

the nature of selfishness itself, you will see that it's nothing but the desire to satisfy your ego, your sense of I'ness, and nothing else.

And when you realize the nature of selfishness, you cease to be selfish yourself. You see the futility of being selfish. And you let go any selfish thoughts as they come to you, and instead become kind and compassionate to others.

When you are kind to a selfish person, it confuses him. He can't understand why you are kind to him. And this makes him question his own selfishness, which if done enough times, helps him overcome his selfishness, and care about others' feelings, too.

This act of replying selfishness with kindness is what we need today to simplify our lives. There is selfishness all around us, but if we all start to be kind to others we may bring a change among others, and they in turn may spread this change.

Imagine what a beautiful world it will be when we can see small acts of kindness everyday in our life. Imagine seeing such acts of kindness all around you – in your home, in your office, on the bus stop.

Start first by being kind yourself, and be the source of kindness in the world, and you will soon start to see the benefits of doing so in your own life, and in the life of others, too.

## Give it a Day

Many times you fall prey to your desires and feelings, and you act upon them and do things, only to regret them the next day.

You buy an expensive phone today, only to find tomorrow that you didn't need it as much as you thought you did. Or, you pick up a fight with your friend, only to find the next day that it wasn't worth fighting for such a small issue.

Such things happen to you again and again. Do you know why?

The reason you do such mistakes is because you act on impulse. And a good way to avoid such situations in future is to not to act at all, and take a break and come back to face your problem the next day.

When you act on impulse, you let your desires and feelings take control over yourself for a few moments. You aren't aware of your actions and their consequences.

What you need then is a break from that situation, so that you can have a fresh look at it later and make the right decision which is the best one for you.

When you give yourself a break for a day, your

desires and feelings lose their grip over you. And when you wake up the next day, after a good night's sleep, you don't feel you want to do something as badly as you did a day before.

When you find yourself in such situation where your impulse seems to take control over you, take a deep breath, let it go, and say to yourself that you will think and act on the problem tomorrow.

You can apply this in many situations.

When you see the ad for the latest smartphone, you may want to instantly order it online. But instead of doing that, take a deep breath, and say to yourself that you'll think about it tomorrow and only then make a decision. And the next day, you'll see that you don't feel as excited to buy it as you felt a day before.

Or, when someone hurts your feelings, you may immediately want to swear at them. But instead of doing that, take a deep breath, and say to yourself that you will tell them what you feel tomorrow. And the next day, you'll find that you don't feel as angry as you felt a day before, and you may even let the matter go.

The same way, you can take a break for a day from every situation in your life where you find yourself acting on impulse and not on careful thought.

So the next time you want to do something badly, give it a day, come back to it tomorrow, and see if you need to do it at all

This has worked well for me many times. Try it and see if it works for you too.

# Do Important Things While Your Mind is Fresh

When you get up at morning, after a good sleep, your mind is more fresh than it is at any other time of the day.

That's why it makes sense to use this fresh mind to do something that makes the best use of it.

Here are a few things I can think of, that do so:

**Meditate**

This is the first thing I suggest you to do. When your mind is fresh, it's easy to focus your full attention on your meditation. As the day passes, your mind gets filled with new information, and then it becomes hard to discard all that information and get back to meditation.

When you sit down to meditate with a fresh mind, you find it easy to concentrate on one object (which may be your breath, your heartbeat, or a thought). The easier your meditation becomes, the more you do it, and the more you learn about yourself.

If you start your day with meditation, even five minutes of practice can help you remain peaceful and mindful for the rest of your day.

**Read**

When your mind is fresh, it's eager to learn new things. And what better way to feed your mind than to fill it with something that you want to fill it with.

You can use this time to read books that you find meaningful. You can read books on meditation, spirituality, or personal growth. When you read with a fresh mind, you understand what's written in the book more clearly and deeply.

If you are a student, you can use this time to learn new things. With a fresh mind you are likely to learn in less time, with less efforts.

**Think**

This is also a good time to think of new ideas or to reflect upon the deeper issues in your life. You can use this time to focus your mind to make important decisions in your life. A fresh mind is the best friend you've got with you to help you make the right choices in life.

When your mind is fresh, you can make better decisions and see all aspects of an action, which you may miss if you take your decisions at a time when your mind is filled with other thoughts to think of.

**Create**

Another good way to make use of your fresh mind, is to create something. If you are a writer, you can write something. If you are a painter, you can paint something. This is the best time of the day to create something, as a fresh mind is open to all possibilities, and you are likely to come up with creative thoughts and ideas.

You also get more done in less time. And you can work deeply on your problems. As your mind is fresh, you can easily identify mistakes when you see them, and this helps you produce high quality work. That's why it's a great time for every artist or creative to work on something new.

**Use your time wisely…**

While these are some of the best ways to make use of your fresh mind, it's also necessary during this time to avoid things that add no value to your life, and simply waste your time – things like social media, email, news, tv, music, or any kind of entertainment that you only use to please your senses.

You can do all such things at later time of your day, when you need to take a break, or when you have some free time to spare. But when your mind is fresh, don't waste it on such useless things. They are not worth it.

The best use of your mind is to do things that help you understand, learn, and improve your life in some way. Those are the things you should do when your mind is still fresh.

# Put Your Family First

What do you do when you have to choose between your family and your work?

Do you choose your family? Or, do you ignore them and focus only on your work?

We often take our family for granted. And even within our family, there are few people whom we always take for granted. We think they'll always be there for us, always ready to help us and do whatever we want them to do.

But are you there for them, too, all the time? Can they count on you whenever they need you? If not, then it's time you start to take your responsibility towards your family seriously, and put their needs before yours.

When we are kids or in our teens, we are selfish. We want everything for ourself. Our needs come before the needs of our family. Our parents have to often remind us how much they do for us, and how little we do for them in return.

But as we grow up, and as we start to spend more and more time with the outside world, we realize that it's not as kind and forgiving to us as our family is. We realize that others don't give a damn about our feelings and interests. And this fact is hard to digest.

It's then that we realize the value of our family. We see how our family always stood behind us. Whether it's your mother, father, brother, sister, uncle, or aunt, someone is always there to support you and love you in spite of your weaknesses.

Our family takes care of our needs, and helps us move ahead in life even in situations when no one else supports us.

For most of us, whatever we become in life is thanks to the care and support of our family. That's why it's not just a formality, but our duty to take care of our family when they need us most. And if that means letting go your work or your personal goals for the greater good of the family, then let it be so.

Put your family first. And your own work and your ego second.

# Live the Right Way

Is there anything in your life that you wish you can undo?

Do you feel angry about yourself for making the wrong choices in life? Do you feel guilty about something you did, that you wish you hadn't done? Do you regret not doing enough for someone you loved or cared for?

If you do, then we have a lot in common, and so I'd like to share with you what helps me to make the right choices in life, and what takes me closer to understand the meaning of life.

When we are kids, our parents teach us what's right and what's wrong to do. Then our teachers take that place. And then we rely on some mentor, coach, or self-help book, to show us the way to live.

There is nothing wrong with such upbringing, and for most of us this is how we form our definition of what's the right way to live.

But, what I've learned from my own experience is that, you have to figure out your own right way of living your life. And this right way is the one which is in perfect harmony with every thing: your own nature, the nature of every living being, the nature of this world, and the nature of this universe.

You have to work hard to form this frame of mind which will guide you to do the right thing in any situation, however difficult it may be. And it almost always takes a lot of pain, depression, anger, and suffering to figure this out.

But that's how you learn it. When you take the easy way, and look for a quick-fix solution, you halt your growth in life. If you blindly follow the advice of one person after another, you'll never discover your own right way.

Also, the right way isn't something you invent in your mind, but something that you discover within, and you'll know the right answers to life the moment they come to you. You won't have any 'Ifs' or 'Buts' about following that way.

You don't know what's right to do and what's wrong to do because of ignorance. Please note, by ignorance, I don't mean you are not intelligent or anything like that. You can be mentally superior to others yet ignorant on the basic rules of life.

Ignorance is the lack of understanding about the true nature of life. We are ignorant because we already have a perception about every thing in life, and we rarely try to challenge this perception. And because of that we can only see our life in limited ways, and not as a part of a whole. True knowledge isn't perceptive, it's universal in nature.

Once you have the valid knowledge you would know what's the right thing to do under any given situation.

Now the question comes, how can you cultivate this knowledge and understanding.

You can proceed step by step.

First, **you have to let go your ego**. Your ego is the biggest obstacle to learning anything new. When your ego makes you think that you already know everything there is to know, you won't learn anything further in life.

But, when you remove your ego, and see things without a biased mind, you see the reality of everything. You see the reality of the nature of everything around you. You see the reality of what's meaningful and what's not. You see the reality of your own body and mind. You see the reality of the present moment, for what it is, and not how it's meant to be or how it should have been.

After you let go your ego, **study the life of great masters**. Learn about life from those who have lived it the right way. Read about the life of Rama, the life of Buddha, and similar great people who lived their whole life on strong principles of morality, kindness, and wisdom. Learn from those whom you respect deeply, and in whose footsteps you want to walk.

Study their life in detail. Study their teachings in detail. Study how they learned what they learned in their life. Study the teachings of the guru or masters that they followed. If you do all this, you'll start to see the thinking, the feeling, and the way these great people have lived their lives, and you'll start to realize how you, too, can walk the path that they walked, and how you, too, can live a life on the same values and principles as they lived.

This will awake a new understanding within you, that'll help you to understand what's right and wrong for yourself.

Then what remains for you is to deepen this understanding more and more, by reading, understanding, and practicing more and more of what you read. This will set you up with the right frame of mind.

The next step, is to **meditate on their teachings**. When you come across any thought that shakes you from within, then meditate upon it for a while. Try to understand that thought as thoroughly as you possibly can. Think of it for the next few minutes, or the next few hours, if you need to do so.

Meditate every day on such great thoughts. And meditate with all your heart. Meditation will help you deepen your understanding about what you read. It will also help you to discover the unknown universal truths about life on your own.

The longer you practice these three steps, (1) Letting go your ego, (2) Studying teachings of great people, and finally, (3) Meditating on these teachings, and the more sincerely you follow each of them, the faster you will make your progress in understanding about life.

To understand the right way to live, you have to begin with the right practice. The above 3 steps will take care of the right practice. You just have to do them every day now.

When we are born, we don't know the meaning of life and the right way to live. But we can work towards understanding that, before we die.

# Just Breathe

Take a breathe and relax.

Whenever you find yourself losing control, just breathe.

Whenever you find yourself jealous of others, just breathe.

Whenever you find yourself acting selfishly, just breathe.

Whenever you feel stressed, just breathe.

Take short breaths, take long breaths, take normal breaths, but just breathe.

Breathe the way you want, but just breathe.

Let go everything you are holding, let go every thought you are thinking, let go every desire you are feeling, and just breathe.

Let go all your senses, and just breathe.

Breathe is the essence of life.

Breathe is what separates life from death.

So, just breathe.

When life doesn't seem to make any sense, just

breathe.

When life makes perfect sense, just breathe.

If you want to find the answers to all your questions, just breathe.

If you can't find the answers to your questions, just breathe.

Breathe away your problems.

Breathe away your fears.

Breathe away your anger.

Breathe away your worries.

Every problem, every fear, every doubt will go away, if you just breathe.

Simply close your eyes, and just breathe.

Let go the future, let go the past. Live in the now, and just breathe.

Life will become so much peaceful, if you just breathe.

Life will become so much joyful, if you just breathe.

Life will become so much simple, if you just breathe.

Stop reading this now, and just breathe.

# Get Rid of Negative Thoughts

We have to deal with negative thoughts and negative people regularly in our life.

Negative thoughts are not only bad for your mood, but also for your health.

Negative feelings hurt friendships, relationships and make you feel bad from inside.

Negative thoughts often lead to anger, and you may end up doing something that you regret later. And they can also cause stress and headaches.

So even though we know that such negative thoughts and feelings aren't good for us, then why do we still continue to to act and think negatively?

The reason is, in reality, it's not easy to transform a negative thought into positive one. We are human beings with thoughts and emotions, and it takes time to change our behavior and actions.

But with the right understanding this can be done. Forget about changing negative thoughts into positive ones. It's hard to be positive-minded when you are burning with negative energy from inside.

What works much better is to prevent this negative

feelings altogether, without letting them affect us in any way.

How can we do this?

To answer this question, lets go a little deeper and analyze the root cause of negativity.

The root cause of all our negativity are those negative thoughts that we have in our mind. All those negative thoughts combine together and make us a negative-minded person, who acts accordingly and causes harm to himself and others.

The truth is, each and every thought arises first in the mind. When any thought enters your mind, be it positive or negative, you have a choice.

A choice to recognize it or act thoughtlessly on it. You must always try to recognize if it's a positive or negative thought, knowing that if it's a negative thought it's going to harm you.

After recognizing the negative thought, it's not necessary to act on it. Ask yourself is it really worth your time and energy to think more about it? Or is it better to let it go and continue with what you were doing?

Once you recognize that a thought is negative, you can let it go. If it comes again, recognize it and let it go again. Never allow it to grow upon you. Never feed that thought by getting involved with it and spending your time thinking about it.

So the next time you start thinking negatively, stop

right there. See what led you to thinking negatively. Each and every time the culprit is a single negative thought that keeps growing inside you, leading you to take wrong actions.

The key is to recognize that first negative thought that comes to your mind, and then let it go.

Most of the time we are not aware that we have a choice, because we are used to acting on impulse rather than on careful observations.

For example, someone insults you and you immediately insult them back; someone blames you and you immediately start defending yourself; if a kid doesn't listen to you, you immediately become angry and start scolding him.

It's tough not to act on impulse as we don't have time to think too much about trivial stuff.

But are they really trivial? Even when they affect your physical and mental well-being on a daily basis?

If you let those negative thoughts overcome you, your life will become miserable.

The good news is, with the right understanding, you can recognize these negative thoughts and eliminate them permanently from your life.

It sounds so simple. Right?

Still most of us continue to act negatively, because we don't filter thoughts as right and wrong, as negative and positive. If you could just filter them then you will see that you have complete power to get rid of them or to act on them.

One thing that can greatly help you in recognizing these thoughts is meditation. By meditating, you become aware about your thoughts and start living in the present moment. You recognize a thought as soon as it comes to your mind.

By practicing meditation regularly, you will be able to control your thoughts and actions in much better way, and will be able to make the right choice when a negative thought comes to your mind.

It takes time and effort to become good at this, but once you start seeing the benefits, you will find that it's worth all the effort.

To overcome negativity, take these actions and start living in the present moment, completely aware of those thoughts that come to your mind.

With time you will be able to get rid of those negative thoughts permanently.

# Stop Worrying

As human beings we have highly developed brains, and with this we often think too much about certain events in our life, and end up harming ourselves in the process.

We worry about past events that happened in our life.

We worry about future events that are yet to happen.

The root cause of this worry is that we think too much about an issue; thinking more than it deserves to be thought about.

We worry about our job.

We worry about our relationship.

We worry about our bank balance.

When all these problems are solved, we start worrying about the unknown, even those events that are not likely to happen.

What happens when we worry so much?

We burden our minds with unwanted tension and feel stressed out.

We are not able to make right decisions when our mind is clouded by such worrying thoughts.

So how can we stop worrying altogether?

If you have the habit of thinking too much about trivial issues in your life, then it will take you some time to give up this habit of worrying.

While certain issues do need your direct attention and needs to be solved with clear thinking, being worried about it isn't going to decrease your burden in any way. You have to understand this.

A better way to spend that time would be to take actions that will really help in decreasing this burden in your mind.

For example, say you are worried about an important job interview tomorrow. Now you can handle this situation in two ways.

First, by thinking too much about the outcome of the interview. What if I fail in this interview? What if I don't meet the employer's expectations? What if I fail to get up in the morning? What if the alarm clock fails to ring?

There is no end to such worrying. If you think about it for some time, you too will realize that you cannot control most of these situations. Sure, you can take some precautions on your side. But can you really eliminate every stumbling block in your way by just thinking about it?

No.

If there is one thing that I have learned from discarding such thoughts, it's that in the long run they don't matter at all.

So how do you tackle such worrying situations?

That's by taking the second way, which is nothing but taking real actions to solve your problems.

Let's go back to our example and see how we can better handle this interview problem.

Instead of worrying about how the interview goes, how about practicing some mock interviews with your friends or family members? Instead of speculating whether the interviewer would ask you such and such questions, how about finding their answers and practice speaking them fluently?

Instead of worrying about failure, how about recognizing this as a great learning experience that might help you in getting an even better job in future?

You see, the whole attitude through which we solve such problems lies in our mind itself. You only have to understand it, and figure out how to channel your thinking in a positive and action-oriented direction.

It might be tough initially, but with a little practice you will start seeing the improvements in your day-to-day life.

If you want to take just one thing away from this article, take this : The next time any worrying thought comes to your mind, then instead of thinking too much about it, take real action towards solving it.

That's all you need to know to solve all those trivial

worries in your day-to-day life, that are nothing but the creations of your mind.

The habit of taking real actions to solve your life problems will help you eliminate those worrying thoughts completely.

# Let it Go

Every now and then, you come in contact with different emotions and feelings inside you.

Some emotions and feelings are good for your physical and mental well-being. You should always welcome such thoughts and emotions that encourage positive actions and motivate you to do something good. Emotions that normally trigger such positive reactions inside you are love, kindness, compassion, and faith.

If some emotions cause positive reactions, then certain emotions also cause negative reactions inside you. Instead of making you feel better, they harm your physical and mental well-being. Emotions that normally trigger such negative reactions inside you are hatred, selfishness, anger, and jealousy.

What to do when you are surrounded by such negative feelings and emotions?

The more you think upon them and feed them, the more they will grow and damage your inner well-being.

When such negativity manifests your mind, it is best not to spend too much time absorbed in it, and just let it go.

Your hatred won't last for long time, if you just let it go.

You don't have to act selfishly, if you just let it go.

Any form of anger will subside, if you just let it go.

Any form of jealousy will cease to exist, if you just let it go.

To let go, first, you need to have the right understanding about these negative actions. You need to have the knowledge that every bad deed done to you by someone, harms the doer more than it harms you.

When you let go any negative feeling, you become free from its grip, and it can't harm you anymore. But when a person does any harm to another innocent person, he cannot easily let it go, as deep inside he knows he is the one who did a wrong act.

To solve any problem the best solution is to understand the root cause of the problem, and take actions that will prevent it from arising all together.

The second best solution is to stop worrying about the problem and just letting it go.

We have to use this second solution sometimes, especially when we are very busy in doing our work, and we don't have enough time to reflect upon the root cause of such problems.

When you are running out of time and can't afford to

think upon such negative thoughts to find their solutions, just take a breathe and let them go.

Letting go, you will come to peace with yourself.

Letting go, you will will be the greater one.

Letting go, you will be the righteous one.

Letting go, you will be the free one.

# Understand and Overcome Greed

In our quest to become a good human being, we have to face a tough enemy called greed.

Greed is nothing but the endless desire to get more and more things in life. Greed is what dictates our actions and thoughts, if we aren't cautious enough. It's greed that tells you to grab that larger piece of pie, or that bigger pack of chips.

Greed is thinking about yourself most of the time, without caring about what the other person feels. Greed destroys friendships, relationships, and is the root cause of bigger mankind troubles like war and corruption.

If you don't control and become aware of it, your greed will only increase with each passing day. And even if you fulfill your every desire you won't be able to live a happy life, because it's the nature of greed to desire for another wish as soon as one wish is fulfilled.

Greed doesn't have any limit. If you think having a big house or a room full of money will satisfy your greed, you're wrong. Even if you get that, you'll want an even bigger house and more money.

Greed is dangerous not just for you, but for our whole human race, and every life on this planet. The plants, animals, and natural resources we have here are limited. If we don't control our greed, we'll end up destroying this beautiful planet.

It's simply impossible to fulfill every person's wish on this planet.

But you may ask if we can't fulfill our wishes and if we can't satisfy our greed, won't that make us unhappy?

There is a good news. Greed cannot be satisfied, but yes it can be controlled. You can control your desires, and yet live a happy, peaceful and satisfied life.

And no, that doesn't mean you have to keep low goals in life, or kill your dreams. It only means to understand what you need, and what you don't.

But before you overcome your greed, you have to understand it's true nature. Why greed arises in your mind? What makes us want that bigger piece of pie? Why we act greedily again and again?

Greed needs an object of desire, something you must have once you've seen it. This object of desire can be anything – a chocolate, drugs, gadgets, member of opposite sex, or just a larger piece of pie.

The object doesn't matter; it's the intention that matters. And overcoming greed means to overcome this intention that arises, whenever you see a desirable object.

Try a small experiment.

Imagine your object of desire is in front of you. It can be anything – choose one that means the most to you. Imagine how it would feel if you had it right now? How would you consume it? How you'll feel after consuming it?

Now as you're imagining this, try to observe your mind at the same time – How your mind reacts when it sees a desirable object? What your mind thinks when you consume those objects in your imagination? How your mind sends you to a fantasy land away from reality? How it makes you react as if you really have that object?

From these observations, can you guess what it is that makes you act greedily?

If not, here is the answer – It's your mind that makes you greedy and forces you to perform those actions to fulfill your greed. The purpose of this little experiment is to tell you that it's not your body that needs those things; it's your mind that makes you think so.

Your hands are not greedy when they try to grab an object; your tongue is not greedy when it enjoys eating; your eyes are not greedy when they want to see something beautiful. The only thing that makes your body act this way is your mind.

It's as simple as that. There is no mystery, no external research needed to prove it. You can do this research on your own, and get to know firsthand how your mind tricks you into having those objects. And you can do this simply by observing your mind.

Controlling your mind is the key to control your greed.

So, let's try to understand this process in detail.

When you see your object of desire in front of you, your eyes see it first, but it's your mind that recognizes that object. Once recognized, the mind tells you to have that object. And then you take action – like pick up that pie and eat it – to fulfill what your mind says.

If you don't do that action, you'll feel incomplete in some way. Because your mind tells you to do it, and you didn't do it. So there is a conflict inside you that makes you uncomfortable. That's why when some friend takes something you want, you remember that for long time, because your mind makes you feel that you have been deprived of something that should've been yours.

Your mind makes you cling desperately to your objects of desire. If you have to overcome greed you've to accept that there is greed inside you. You have to remain alert for any situations in which you act greedily. Only then can you overcome greed.

So, let's see how we can overcome greed, with an example.

Suppose you are with a group of friends, having pizza. And one piece is significantly larger than all other pieces. What happens now?

Your mind tells you to grab that larger piece, as it knows you like that pizza. And if you take that larger piece, you can enjoy it for longer time. So you go ahead and take that piece, eat it, and later even forget about it.

This cycle continues every time, whenever you face the same situation. If you were to hang out with your friends for the rest of your life, you would do the same thing again and again. Even if you allow others to have it, you won't feel happy from inside.

But the problem is this greed isn't limited to a piece of pie. It attaches itself with every little thing you desire that's supposed to make you happy; happy for only a few moments, not any longer than that.

So to overcome greed, we've to stop ourself from acting, the moment a selfish thought comes to our mind. So as soon as the thought to grab a desirable object comes to your mind, stop right there. Don't take any action. Just observe your mind at that moment.

Just see what your mind is forcing you to do. And once you become aware that you are being greedy, let that thing go, and instead choose the option that does justice to others too.

Again when greed arises, do this same thing. Stop the moment you realize you are being greedy, understand the greed inside you, let it go, and then choose the option that's best for everyone.

When you practice this way for few times, you'll realize that you always had the choice to choose between greed and generosity. It's only that you never knew you had that choice.

Your mind was conditioned to make you act greedily. This conditioning can be caused by several factors – your upbringing, your society, your friends, and even self-learned.

Whatever the reason, the solution is the same. And when you do this for few times, you'll be able to do it every time. Most humans aren't greedy by nature. It's the world that makes them so, and partly they become so due to their own ignorance.

I known how many times I've acted greedily in my life. Only now I realize that it was due to ignorance, and nothing else. I thought only about myself while making those choices. It's only when I grew up and started seeing kindness all around me, that I realized my mistake and thankfully, learned to let things go.

I can't tell you how happier it makes you when you let go of greed completely. Sure it isn't possible to give everything in life. And you'll cherish some possessions and experiences. But you'll never do it at the cost of others' happiness.

Giving up greed is among the best things that happened to me as I grew up. And if you're like me in any way, then it'll be among the best things that could happen to you.

Your life will become more peaceful, happier, and

satisfactory, when you give up greed in every aspect of your life. Be it friendship, relationships, or people you've never met, you'll want nothing from anyone.

Learn to overcome greed, and you'll be on your way towards living a more meaningful life.

# Spend Some Time Alone Every Day

We all live a busy life. We all have our own responsibilities to carry out every day.

It doesn't matter whether you are a student, employee, or manager – there is no one who doesn't have his own burdens.

Add to this the events that happen every day in your life which are beyond your control. Your car broke down; your senior yelled at you; you failed at your task; and sometimes more than one thing can go wrong.

And that's when you feel depressed, and blame your situation on such and such persons or conditions. You do that because it's easy to blame others for your sufferings; what's hard is to accept the truth and take actions to improve your life.

But to take the right actions, you need to understand what's right and what's not. And for that, you need time to find the right answers for all your questions. That's why you need to form this habit of spending some quiet time alone every day.

If you want to live a meaningful life, learn to apply

this every day in your life. Spend some quality time sitting alone, quietly, and reflecting upon the events in your life.

The more time you spend reflecting upon the events in your life, the better you'll understand them. The better you understand them, the better you can handle them.

Take some time out of your daily life and reflect upon the events of the present or previous day. You can do this any time you are free. Usually early morning and just before you sleep at night works best for most people.

Think about the things that are happening in your life right now. Ask yourself questions, and answer them honestly. There is no one to give you good grades for the best answer. Just be honest with yourself.

Ask yourself – why that person treated you in wrong way? why did this happen to you and not to somebody else? what can you do to make sure that it doesn't happen again? how can you become strong to handle such situations in future?

There may be a hundred different questions like this, but do ask yourself the most important questions every day and try to find their answers. And when you do find the answers try to implement them in your daily life.

Reflecting every day on your thoughts is a good habit, and like any other habit you need to practice it daily to reap its benefits for long time. When you reflect on your life every day, you understand more and more about it with each passing day.

You recognize your strengths and understand your weaknesses. You gain more control over your actions. You learn to identify the right from wrong, and are able to make the right choice even when you are provoked to do the wrong thing.

In short, you start gaining inner mastery.

It won't be long before you start to ask yourself more and more deeper questions about life; Questions that arise only out of deep thinking and which can only be answered by deep thinking; Questions that matter much much more than those superficial level questions you had earlier.

But that's something you'll figure out later when you face them. For now, it's enough to get started with this habit of reflecting every day on your thoughts and feelings. And to do that you have to spend some quiet time daily.

You can't think clear thoughts, at least not when you are just starting out, when there are other people around you. You can't think clearly when there is lot of noise, pollution and chaos around you.

You can only think clearly if you are at a quiet and peaceful place, all on your own, with no one to disturb you or interrupt your smooth flow of thoughts and feelings. When these thoughts and feelings flow inside you, you learn to see them clearly and analyze them properly.

Then you gain all the knowledge you need to make the right decisions, if the same situation were to come up again.

That's how you learn to grow every day – both personally and professionally. Just one good habit and you are on your way towards living a better life.

Life is a beautiful journey. Don't let it turn ugly by filling it with bad experiences. Instead, take actions when you have the time, do the right things when you have the choice, and spend some time alone when you have the chance.

# Find the Root Cause of Your Personal Problems

Many times, we ignore our personal problems and move on with our life, as if ignoring our problems will make them go away.

And sometimes, we are so afraid of our problems that we try to hide from them, and avoid doing anything that may make us come face-to-face with them.

So, let's accept it. It's not easy to face your problems, especially those that affect you deeply inside.

But you can't live a peaceful life, when your problems are running at the back of your mind.

If you don't solve your problems today, they'll only become more difficult to face tomorrow.

The best way I know to overcome my problems is to meditate deeply upon them, and find their root cause.

Solving your problems at a surface level never helps you get rid of them. You have to find a way to solve your life's problems permanently, or else they'll keep returning to you again and again. And to solve your problems permanently, first, you have to find their root cause.

To find the cause of your problems, start by asking yourself the right questions: Why do my problems occur? What is their source? What can I do to overcome them?

And when you try to find the cause of your problems, be honest with yourself.

Once you understand the root cause of your problem, you also realize what you're doing wrong, and what you should actually do, to overcome the problem in future.

Let's see an example where finding the root cause can help you overcome the problem.

Suppose your problem is: You want to meditate daily, but for some reason you don't do it.

Now, how do you solve this problem?

First, let's try to find the root cause of your problem. Ask yourself why you don't meditate. List out all possible reasons.

These may be few of the important reasons:

1) You don't have time.

2) You don't know the right/best way to meditate.

3) You don't have the quiet/perfect environment around you to practice.

Now, once you have the root cause of your problems, it becomes easy to figure out a solution. And most times, the solution is simple, though it may not be an easy one.

And the solutions to our meditation problems are also simple:

Problem: You don't have time.

Solution: Really? You mean you can't take just 2-5 minutes from your daily routine to meditate. You can wake up 5 minutes early, reduce your tv or internet time, practice it before you go to sleep; it's not that hard.

Problem: You don't know the right/best way to meditate.

Solution: Start with what you know. All you need to know to meditate is to focus on your breathe and let go everything else. First get better at this, or choose any of the other meditation techniques, and then worry about the best practices later.

Problem: You don't have the quiet/perfect environment around you to practice.

Solution: Well, if you wait for the perfect place or time to meditate, you'll never ever meditate. Start with where you are, with what you have. With enough practice, you'll be able to meditate even in noisy environments.

You see, how simple these solutions are. Finding the root cause of your problems makes you realize that your problems aren't that difficult to overcome at all.

Any problem, however big it may be, can always be solved if you just take the required efforts to find its root cause, and then take actions to eradicate those root causes permanently from your life.

It's difficult, I know. But it's doable. And it's always worth it.

On the other hand, if you don't solve your problems, you let them gain power over you. And the longer you let that happen, the more powerful your problems become.

But once you decide to meditate upon them, and find their root cause, you understand them for what they are. And then you can choose to stand up, look them in the eye, and take the necessary action to overpower them, until your problems go away permanently.

And then you can move to another problem, and then another, and a day will soon come when you won't have any problem left to solve.

# Be Peaceful from Inside

Have you ever lost your self-control only to regret it later? Do you get instantly angry when someone contradicts or abuses you? Do you get mad about people or events on which you have no control?

Don't worry. We all go through such situations in life. We often lose our self-control and act impulsively, instead of thoughtfully, and end up regretting our actions, only wishing that we should've handled the situation in a more mature way.

We become angry, act impulsively, and defend our actions and emotions because we let other people and events affect us and disturb our inner peace.

But when you are at peace with yourself, other people and outer circumstances cannot affect you. By being peaceful you learn to *act*, and not *react* to situations.

Every minute of your day is then an action that you choose to do, instead of a reaction that you regret doing later. So even if someone abuses you, you can choose to ignore the person or talk calmly with him, instead of reacting and abusing him back.

And you can only do this if you are completely peaceful from inside.

You should strive to make yourself so peaceful within, that no amount of inner or outer chaos can have any affect on you. Let this peacefulness show itself in every thought you think and every action you perform.

When you are totally calm inside, you remain unaffected even when there is lot of noise, crowd, or people fighting around you. This benefit alone tells us how strong we become from inside, when we act every waking moment with peace.

And that's not the only benefit you gain from being peaceful.

When you are at peace, you don't make hasty decisions. Every action that you take, every word that you speak, and every thought that you entertain in your mind is based on deep thinking and introspection, which comes only if you are quiet from inside.

You become more kind, more forgiving, less selfish, and more understanding than you were before.

And this happens because you are in such a quiet state that you can observe your thoughts come and go in your mind. So you are able to instantly recognize a disturbing thought, discard it and return back to your calm state.

But this state of deep calmness doesn't come easily. This is because we've conditioned ourselves to think and react all the time. And it'll take some time to break these old patterns and form new ones.

I too struggle with staying peaceful all the time. But by practicing regularly, I can now sense abundance of peace inside me for most part of the day. And I am sure you too can feel the same, if you just practice enough.

Also remember, being peaceful starts with yourself. Don't expect others around you to become a peaceful person, just because you've become one. Else you'll be only disappointed and fall back to your old ways of thinking and reacting.

Your friends and family won't change, unless you do. You need to become the one, who others can follow and learn from.

And when you live your life and perform your everyday actions with a sense of calmness, you are bound to make others and yourself happy.

By being a peaceful person, you reduce the negativity around you. And as a side-result you also inspire others to become as peaceful as you.

And in this peaceful state, you start enjoying the little things in life to which you didn't pay any attention earlier.

You feel joy when you see children playing, birds chirping, and flowers swaying in wind. Even seeing little acts of kindness makes you immensely happy.

What made you angry before, won't be able to disturb your inner peace anymore. What made you impulsively react before, will cease to have any affect on you now.

You will be living peace, practicing peace, and breathing with peace all the time.

And when you are in such peaceful state is there even a possibility of chaos or anger to enter inside you? Absolutely not.

With regular practice you'll be able to be at peace even with your own thoughts. Whenever any thought will pop in your mind, you'll be able to instantly recognize it, and decide whether you should entertain and go along with it, or just let it go.

And as you keep doing that you'll become more calm and compassionate than you have ever been. And that's something that benefits not only you, but everyone else around you.

Next, you'll find the steps you need to take to become a peaceful person.

# Become a Peaceful Person

There are several benefits of being a peaceful person.

When you are at peace, you feel happy and content from inside. Your mind becomes less noisy, and your thoughts and actions are more stable and purposeful.

To become peaceful, all you need to do is create the right conditions, and peace will automatically find its way inside you.

So now, I'd like to share with you the steps that actually helped me become a peaceful person. And I'm sure they will work for you, too, if you just give them enough time to sync deeply inside you.

All these are practical tips that you can start applying right now as you read this. And then keep applying them everyday to become more and more peaceful with each passing day.

So let's start with them one by one.

**Let go your ego**

By ego, I don't mean just your pride, but your sense of thinking about everything around you in terms of 'I'. Normally, you define yourself based on what you think, act, and feel. But that's not who you really are.

Your thoughts and actions are a result of the way you have conditioned your mind since childhood. So even if your thoughts and actions change with time, you still remain the same person as you have always been. When you think in terms of "This happened to me", "He did that to me", "This belongs to me", you let your ego win and misguide you by suggesting you the wrong actions.

But when you let go your ego – your sense of 'I'ness – you start seeing people and events as they really are. You don't see them as per your opinion or your experience, but just as they naturally exist. And when you realize that, you'll no longer respond to people and events as you earlier did. You'll have nothing to fight about, nothing to worry about, and nothing to change about yourself or others.

**Let go your thoughts**

It's the nature of our mind to jump from one thought to another continuously. An uncontrolled mind alone is enough to disturb your peace. If you keep jumping from one thought to another, your mind can never become still, and without stillness there can be no peace.

So when random thoughts come to you, don't entertain them, don't give them any value, and they will pass away soon. The problem arises when you keep indulging yourself into one thought after another. Stop indulging in those thoughts and you'll see yourself getting more and more quiet within.

While letting go your thoughts, your goal should not be to force your mind to go into a thoughtless state, but to watch your thoughts simply as an observer without getting attached to them. And let those thoughts arise, stay, and leave your mind without affecting you in any way.

When thoughts cease to exist, the mind also returns to its natural peaceful state.

**Let go your desires**

Desires are the root cause of all our unhappiness. The biggest problem with our desires is that they are never satisfied. One desire always leads to another. When you get what you desire you start desiring something better, and when you get that too, you desire something still better. This is the true nature of our desires.

But desires have no place in the heart of a peace-loving person. Having desires means there is something lacking in your life. And when you lack something how can you remain happy and peaceful? You can't.

By letting go your desires you give up living a future imagined state of happiness, which doesn't exist, and you start living the present beautiful moment, which does exist.

**Remove existing attachments**

When you give up desires you feel content with what you have. And that sure is a good thing, but if you get too attached with your existing conditions then that too is a kind of desire – a desire for not wanting to change.

For example, even if you give up your desire to own a big house, but can't give up your attachment towards your existing house, then that too is a desire that must be uprooted.

One by one remove all your existing attachments. When there are no desires for future conditions and no attachments to existing conditions, peace automatically finds its way into your heart.

**Be mindful all the time**

Letting go your ego, thoughts and desires isn't supposed to be a one time exercise which you only practice for few minutes a day. It's supposed to be a state of living which you should try to be in every moment you are awake. And to live in this state you have to be mindful of everything in and around you, all the time.

By being mindful throughout the day you never leave your guard and can sense as soon as any disturbance arises inside you. And once you recognize these unwanted disturbances, you can discard them peacefully and then return back to keeping your guard.

Thus practicing mindfulness helps you remain in a peaceful state, all the time.

**Meditate as often as you can**

Meditation helps you understand more and more about yourself. You understand the workings of your mind, and the nature of your thoughts and feelings.

Meditation also helps you find answers to all your questions for yourself, without depending on anyone else. And if you mediate on what I've just said you can figure out for yourself whether it's true or not.

Meditation will help you gain the knowledge, you need to know, to become peaceful. Meditation will help you gain the ability, you need to have, to remain peaceful. Meditation itself will bring deep peace whenever you practice it.

That's all you need to know to become a peaceful person.

All that remains now for you is to understand what you've just read, test for yourself if it's true, and then practice it every day.

Becoming peaceful is a choice – either you take the right efforts to become peaceful or you continue to live in chaos.

And it does take time and effort to apply these changes in your everyday life. But once you start to experience the benefits for yourself, you'll be happy you made these changes in your life.

# Be Still

Everywhere we go, there seems to be chaos around us. Everything seems to be moving so fast, and we often find ourselves failing to catch up with the world.

Whenever you find yourself in such chaos, try to become still from inside. Be still and enjoy the stillness.

Don't move. Don't think. Don't try to feel anything. Just remain still.

When you see everyone around you rushing through their day and chasing meaningless goals, pause and reflect upon your own life. You don't have to rush through your life. You can do your work and complete your goals even by remaining calm and peaceful throughout the day.

When you become totally still from inside, the outside world also seems to become less noisy and less chaotic.

When others see you remain calm, they too feel a sense of calmness within them. Your quietness makes them want to become quiet themselves.

Stillness brings peace. It brings clarity. It removes all

your doubts and confusions.

Stillness helps you declutter your mind. Stillness turns your chatty mind into a peaceful one, and it turns those tons of unimportant thoughts into a few important ones.

Stillness always helps you separate the few from many, and the important from the useless ones.

Every once in a while, separate yourself from the crowd. Go to some quiet place and enjoy the stillness around you. Observe the beauty of Nature and learn how everything looks so beautiful when it's quiet and content with itself.

See the flowers and trees and try to become as still as them. This will help you return to your original nature which is peaceful, loving, and full of kindness.

When your mind becomes calm and quiet, life becomes so much easier, life becomes so much beautiful, and life becomes so much simple.

By practicing stillness you can have better self-control and it will give you the power to remain quiet within, even when there is chaos outside. And you also gain the ability to make others calm when they seem to be losing themselves.

Stillness has power. By being still, you gain the power to think your thoughts more clearly. You gain the power to separate the right thoughts from the wrong ones. And this gives you the power to do only the right action, and say only the right words.

For example, when the water flows in a lake, you can't see clearly what lies beneath the water. But when the water becomes still you can see everything clearly.

The same way, when your mind becomes still, you can see everything that's inside your mind. You can understand the nature of your mind and how your mind works. You can also see everything that comes and goes out from your mind.

In another example, suppose you take a glass of clean water and mix it with muddy water, then even the clean water becomes muddy. But when you just let that glass become still, the mud gets collected at the bottom of the glass. And the top of glass becomes clean and clear.

The same way, when you have so many thoughts running in your mind, it's difficult to work and think upon all of them at the same time. But when you become still, you can see the unwanted thoughts, discard them, and choose the clean and pure thoughts in your mind.

A still mind can easily recognize the negative thoughts surrounding it. It can easily recognize anger, jealousy, ego, selfishness, and can remain unaffected from them.

If you find it difficult to become still, take the path of meditation.

Meditation will give you the ability to become still anytime you want, anywhere you want, for as much time as you want.

Put aside a time for stillness everyday in your schedule. Enjoy this stillness before you go to work. Enjoy this stillness after you return from work. Even try to live with stillness when you work.

Stillness will make your life more peaceful, more joyful, and more meaningful.

# Find True Happiness in Life

What does happiness mean to you?

Achieving fame, money, goals, desires, possessions?

If so, then no matter what you do, and how hard you work, you'll always find yourself away from happiness. Because what you seek can only give you temporary happiness, and never permanent one.

Each day, from morning to night, we take actions that we think will take us closer to live a happy life.

But, when the day ends, how many of us really feel happy and contented? How many of us feel peaceful from within?.

We live in a culture where we encourage ambitions, greed, and overwork and discourage contentment, selflessness, and rest. We respect ambitious people and look down upon those who are contented with their life.

We think we'll only be happy when we have a high-paying job, a big house, and enough money to fulfill our every little desire.

We always look for something more, and even when we get that, we desire for something even more.

I, too, used to think this way. If any friend told me he is happy with what he has, I tried to convince him how having more in his life will make him more happy than he is now. What a fool I was.

It takes time to realize that our possessions and money have nothing to do with our happiness. And it's even more difficult to understand this, if you are young, as you're struggling to find your own identity in life, and you can't help comparing your life to other rich and successful kids in college.

Money does play a role in our happiness. We do need some money to satisfy our basic needs in life. But anything beyond that, won't necessarily add to your happiness.

Money, possessions, fame, respect, position. All these won't give you happiness. If you have any thoughts that make you think otherwise, then throw them aside.

And ask yourself, how can I be truly happy? And, where does happiness actually come from?

True happiness always comes from within. There is no way it can come from anything outside you. You probably know this, but still look outside for happiness.

If you keep looking for happiness outside, you'll never find it. Happiness comes from a quiet mind, a contented heart, and controlled senses. All this are under your control. And to control them, you have to be mindful of yourself for every moment of your day, and keep your focus directed within.

True happiness can't be bought. It can't be snatched from someone else. It can't be rented. It can't be bribed. It can't be seen. It can't be heard. It can't be tasted. It can't be felt from outside.

True happiness always comes from within and it can be felt only from within. It comes from a state of peacefulness within you that you have to find, understand, and then live by. In this peaceful state, you will find as much happiness as you want. And in it there is no place for any kind of negative energy.

Yes, that means no greed, no jealousy, no anger, no stress. But, pure contentment, pure happiness, pure compassion, and pure peace.

If your definition of happiness lies in things which are outside your control, then you will never be happy in your life. There will always be someone more famous than you, there will always be someone more rich than you, there will always be someone more powerful than you, and there will always be someone more talented than you.

You can only be happy if your definition of happiness lies under your control. You can let go your desires, let go your ego, let go your thoughts, and let go any other thing that doesn't contribute to your happiness. If you can do that, then you won't compare your happiness with others. You will be happy from inside, and you'll feel this deep within.

Now, what tells you that you have truly become happy? You know you are truly happy when you are grateful for all the things in your life, when you are grateful for the kindness others have shown you in your life, and when you are grateful for your food, your house, your family, and the wisdom you have gained in your life.

You know you are truly happy when you know no one in this planet is unhappy because of you, when you respect every life in this planet – be it plant or animal – and you consume only what's necessary to live your life. Then you create happiness not only within you, but also outside you.

When your love and kindness extends beyond yourself, beyond your family, beyond your culture, beyond your country, and you see equality in everything, then you are truly happy to be you, because then there is no difference between you and me and anyone else. We all are same in every respect. We all have desires, goals, thoughts, and love inside us. When you start to live your life based on such universal thoughts, you start to look at life with new eyes. Everything is a thing of beauty then, that exists for its own wonderful reason.

Then you don't feel angry when things don't turn out your way. You don't feel disappointed when you can't own expensive things. You don't care for fame, or position. You respect every life form there is, and with that comes the respect for yourself, too. And you start working on what's more important to you in life. You start to discover the purpose of your own existence. You start to see the inner beauty in you, which is way more beautiful than any outside beauty.

That's how you find true happiness in your life. And once you find it, there is nothing more left to run after.

If my words can help you find this happiness in your life, I will consider myself very fortunate.

# Embrace Loneliness

At times, you'll come across situations in your life where you find yourself alone. There will be moments when you won't have anyone to help you, to pity you, and show any sign of love to you.

It's in moments like these, that we feel shattered and depressed.

We are so used to having others in our life that we find it difficult to deal with ourself when we are alone.

We always want to do something – see something, feel something, go somewhere, read something, talk to someone, listen to something, or work on something.

We don't like it when we have nothing to do, and are left on our own.

But, if you want to know the truth about yourself and understand this world around you, you should start to accept this loneliness in life. And not just accept it, but embrace it with all your heart.

To understand the meaning of life, you have to get rid of the chaos around you, and dwell inside the quietness in you. And this quietness can only be found when you are alone.

It's in moment of loneliness that you feel the sadness and the emptiness in your life. You come face to face with your fears, your desires, your anger, your jealousies, your thoughts, and your feelings. You see them for what they are. And then, if you look deeply, you see yourself for who you are.

You can keep running from the truth as long as you want. You can lose yourself in chasing one desire after another. You can do that for long enough.

But there will come a time, as it mostly does, when you can't run from the truth any longer, and you begin to question your own existence and of everything else around you. For some, such moments come at the end of their lives as they approach their death. For some, it comes early in their lives as they see the suffering and pain around them. For some, unfortunately, the moment never comes, and they leave this world without having understood it.

True learning only comes from independence. Do not depend on others to make you happy all the time. Do not depend on others to care for you all the time. Do not depend on others to make decisions for you all the time. Do not depend on others to guide you all the time.

Learn to be happy on your own. Learn to be decisive on your own. Learn to be careful on your own. Learn to guide yourself on your own. And to learn all these, first, learn to live with your loneliness.

If you are afraid to be alone, and cling to other people or things all the time, then you will never grow up to understand the purpose of your life. You have to let go your fears, be bold, and get away from everything.

Go, find a quiet room or a garden, so that you can sit quietly, close your eyes, meditate, and think upon the important things in your life.

When you meditate on your problems in your loneliness, the magic starts to happen: what was complicated before, becomes simple; what was once difficult, becomes easy; what was impossible before, becomes possible; what seemed important before, becomes trivial; what was useful before, becomes useless; what was chaotic before, becomes calm; what was anger before, becomes peace. All this, and much more happens when you start to live with your loneliness.

Loneliness doesn't mean to shrink away from your duties, or your family and friends. You can do all your duties for the day, spend quality time with your family and friends, and yet make some time every day to be alone. You can make this time before you go to sleep at night, or after you wake up in the morning. You can make this time even when others are around you, by being quiet and focused only on your inner self.

I spend time in loneliness every day. I need this loneliness to figure out what's important to me. I need this loneliness to figure out the purpose of my life. I need this loneliness to create anything of value. And I

am glad I have learned to live with my loneliness.
What about you?

# Live in the Present Moment

When you live in the present moment, all problems vanish.

There is no stress, no anger, no regret; just what's happening now.

To live in the present moment, you have to focus on your current activity and let go every other thought from your mind. Your mind will keep on trying to distract you, but you must stay firm and actively reengage yourself with the present activity.

The present moment is the only moment you have. You cannot control the future. You cannot change the past. But you can control this moment that's happening right now.

Worrying too much about your past and future won't solve your problem. Taking actions in the present moment will.

When you start living in the present moment, there are no regrets of the past and no worries for the future. You are totally immersed in living in this moment and you live your life to the fullest.

But how do you live in the present moment?

First, just relax yourself. Breathe slowly and consciously. Do this for few minutes until you feel completely relaxed.

Now, observe what's going on inside your mind. What thoughts are you thinking right now?

Are you thinking about your past or some future event. If yes, stop right there and continue to focus on your current activity. The only thing that exists at this moment is that activity. Nothing else.

If any thoughts arise in your mind, that are not related to the present moment, discard them completely from your mind. Don't give them any attention. Simply, continue doing your work with full dedication.

You can't change your past just by thinking about it over and over again. And the future will never be as exact as you imagine it. Knowing this will help you when you practice living in the present moment.

To live in the present, you have to let go every thought from your mind that takes you away from the present moment. You don't have to force your mind to reject any unwanted thought. Instead, consider the thought as worthless and simply ignore it.

Our mind has been conditioned to think about our past and future all the time. That's why it needs a lot of practice to break this habit, and to live in the present moment. You can start this practice by doing one thing at a time. When walking, just walk. When listening, just listen. When eating, just eat.

Don't mix two or more activities together. You will end up doing nothing perfectly.

Do one thing at a time and do it with full dedication, as if it's the only thing that exists in the whole universe; the only thing that matters at this moment.

If your mind wanders, bring it back to the present moment. It's the nature of our mind to wander ceaselessly from one thought to another. Every time you become aware of its wandering, bring it back to the present moment.

With practice, you will be able to control your mind from wandering aimlessly. You'll learn that your mind is just a tool to be used, and not something that should totally dictate your life. Then, your actions will be no longer the result of your flickering mind. Your actions will result from conscious thinking.

Your mind won't control you. You will control your mind.

But to do this, you have to first start by living in the present moment.

# Clear Your Mind of Unwanted Thoughts

Often, we find ourselves clouded with tons of thoughts.

Too many thoughts rush to our mind at the same time, and it becomes difficult to pick one thought and focus on it.

To live a peaceful life, it's important that you learn to deal with these thoughts without disturbing your mental balance.

Our mind has limited capacity. If you think too much about too many things at the same time, you will only get stressed out and lose your inner peace.

If this happens, you first need to clear your mind of all the unwanted thoughts, and keep only the useful ones in your mind.

So, how do we clear our mind of unwanted thoughts?

There are two ways I know of that you can use directly. One is simple, other is a bit difficult.

The simple way is to get some sleep.

Sleep is the natural way to relax our mind and give it

some rest. When we are in sleep, the mental chatter going in our mind stops, and we become unconscious of our problems while we are sleeping. This helps the mind to relax and take some rest.

And when you wake up, you will find yourself refreshed, and ready to make a fresh start to solve your problems again.

I can remember so many times when I've struggled with such unwanted thoughts in my mind. But when I just went to sleep and woke up the next day, I could easily understand my problems, and solve them.

And some of those problems didn't even seem as big as they seemed a day ago.

That's how sleep works its magic on us and makes it easier for us to think upon our problems the next day.

You, too, probably know this from your own experience. Try to remember a time when you were tired, or unable to decide between many options, and you went to sleep with a heavy mind. And the next day when you woke up, you felt much more in control of yourself, and solved those problems in no time.

This method works almost all the time. For this method to work, you need to give up your control over your mind and let sleep do rest of the work.

But what if you are in a place where you can't sleep?

And what if you do need to sort out a complicated problem that needs deep thinking, which you can't just solve by going to sleep?

To solve such problems, we need some other method that we can apply anywhere and anytime.

And that other method is to work on your thoughts with awareness.

Actually, this way to solve your problems with awareness is even better than going to sleep, as you are in complete control of yourself and consciously solve your problems as and when they arise.

So let's try to see how to deal with our thoughts with awareness, step by step. Read this slowly, and even better, try to practice it now itself.

First, close your eyes and relax. Make yourself comfortable and let your mind and body completely relax.

For me, deep breathing also helps in speeding up this relaxation process. Just breathe slowly, taking deep breaths, and let your attention rest on your breath for a while.

After a few minutes you should feel very relaxed and peaceful from inside.

Now start working on your thoughts, one by one.

Don't rush yourself. Don't try to go after all your thoughts at the same time.

Just continue to relax, and let your thoughts come automatically to you, one by one. It's most likely that the most troublesome thoughts will come first. Work on whichever thoughts comes first, without forgetting to relax. And if that thought starts troubling you, bring your attention back to your breath.

After few breaths, get back to the problem again and try to solve it again, while keeping yourself totally calm.

If you still can't solve that problem, keep it aside and say mentally to yourself that you'll work on it later.

Now move on to another thought. Work on it the same way. If you think that you don't need to work on that thought right now, then simply let it go. Don't think too much about it. Don't force yourself to not think about it.

Simply witness that thought coming to your mind, staying there, and finally leaving your mind.

Then move on to another thought and so on.

The key here is to work on our thoughts one by one. There is no way you can clear your mind of all unwanted thoughts, if you just keep rushing from one thought to another without giving them enough time to stay, rest, and then leave your mind.

Practicing this simple way of awareness and dealing with one thought at a time, helps you recognize those important thoughts and remove the other unwanted thoughts from your mind.

Start practicing this method whenever you find yourself overwhelmed with too many thoughts. With more and more practice, you'll find that it keeps getting easier every time.

And when your mind becomes clear and calm, you'll automatically feel a sense of peace and happiness in you.

# Make Your Mind Quiet

Our mind never stops thinking.

Every moment of the day, it keeps rushing from one thought to another. It finds it difficult to stay quiet and do nothing.

But that's the very nature of our mind. And we can't blame it for that.

If you leave your mind on its own, it will never become quiet. To make it quiet, you have to take control yourself. And that involves practicing mindfulness and meditation; the two best ways to quiet your mind.

When your mind becomes quiet, you feel peace inside you. This peace is similar to how you feel in any quiet place, except here you feel peaceful at a deeper level. And another great thing about this peace is that it lasts longer.

When the mind is quiet, there are no thoughts, and even when thoughts do come, you can easily discard them and continue to stay in the quietness of your mind.

When the mind becomes quiet, it stops rushing towards your desires, it stops thinking about your ego, and it stops acting as per your senses.

And in this quietness it can do something it couldn't do before: Your mind is able to observe itself. And that's when you start to see the beauty inside you.

In this quietness and peace, you start to feel the 'real' you. This you is not a formation of your mind, nor a creation of your desires. This you is your consciousness, which you didn't know earlier, because it doesn't show itself when your mind is run by desires.

Your consciousness, by its nature, is opposite of your mind. It's naturally quiet and peaceful. And that's why, to know it, you first have to make your mind as quiet as consciousness itself.

As your mind becomes quiet, your consciousness starts revealing itself. At first, it barely seems to be there, but as your mind becomes quieter and quieter, your consciousness starts becoming more and more visible.

Within this quietness, your mind seems to be at so much peace that you don't feel like disturbing it. You wish to remain in this state for more and more time.

And when you come out of this state, you still feel so much peace inside you. The whole world seems to have become peaceful along with you. Everything looks so calm.

As you practice this more often, you start to gain better control over your mind. You immediately recognize any unwanted thought or feeling as soon as it arises. You are able to make better decisions all the time. You are aware of everything in and around you, every moment you are awake.

This state of quietness of mind is a beautiful state to be in.

No wonder, many meditators meditate everyday just to enjoy this state.

But our purpose isn't to do this for enjoyment. If you do this for the joy, then you will easily rush to any other thing that gives you joy.

We make our mind quiet, so that we can understand ourselves at a deeper level. We do this to discover the true nature of everything inside us: our mind, our feelings, our desires, our senses.

This deep understanding helps us clear many doubts about ourself, as well as about life itself. It helps us break free from the many self-imposed limitations that we live with everyday.

It brings us closer to the truth.

So, for today, I'd like you to put away some time, and use meditation to quieten your mind, even if it's just for a few minutes.

# Drink Your Tea with Mindfulness

After you get up at morning, and before you start your day's work, few experiences can be as enriching as drinking a cup of tea with mindfulness.

I enjoy my daily tea routine. It has become like a five-minute-meditation for me. It helps me relax, and refreshes my body and mind, and prepares me to face my day in a peaceful way.

While you should certainly try for yourself what drink – tea or coffee – works best for you, and what way you like to drink it, I'd like to share with you my process of drinking tea.

Here is how to drink your tea with mindfulness:

First, be mindful while making your tea. Don't be in a hurry. Be aware of everything you do: how much water you take, how much tea you put, for how many minutes you let the water boil.

Once you finish making it, immerse yourself completely into the experience of drinking the tea. We are more interested in the drinking part of our tea, than the making part.

I prefer to sit in a quiet place, but it may not be possible for you to find such a place every time.

Whether quiet or noisy, don't let the environment around you distract you from drinking your tea peacefully.

Sit down on a chair, or you can sit down cross-legged on a mat, as I do sometimes, with just your cup of tea.

Bring your attention back to the present moment. Don't think of anything else.

Don't have any books, newspapers, or cell phones near you. Keep them away for a while. You need five to ten minutes to enjoy your tea. And this time is not to be shared with anything else.

Before you take the first sip, enjoy the aroma of the tea. Take a few deep breaths and with each breath let the fresh aroma of the tea fill your body.

Take the first sip slowly, and enjoy it. Don't rush to take the second sip. Let the first sip fully dissolve in your mouth first.

Similarly, take the next sips while being mindful of each sip as you take it. Cherish every sip, and observe it as it dissolves in your mouth and enters your body. Feel the tea inside you, as it moves from your mouth to your stomach.

Take your time. If you need more than five minutes, let it be so. Depending upon how much tea you drink, and how mindfully you drink it, your time may vary from five to fifteen minutes. It's alright. The alertness and the quietness you feel within, is worth the time.

Even when you finish drinking your tea, don't get up

immediately. Spend a few minutes observing the feeling inside you. After a hot cup of tea, it's natural to feel little warm inside, which makes you feel relaxed and peaceful, and yet fully alert.

After this experience, you come out fresh and full of energy to begin your day. This morning experience, enriching as it is, is a great way to begin your day.

And you don't have to limit this experience to once a day. You may do this two or three times a day. Apart from morning, another good time to do this is at evening, after you finish your day's work. Or you can do it anytime you feel stressed during your day. Whether evening or noon, drink your tea with the same mindfulness as you do at morning.

You can have any type of tea you prefer. It's a matter of personal choice. I prefer to take green tea, without milk or sugar, one to two times a day. There are several health benefits of drinking green tea over other types of tea, and I highly recommend it to you.

Every time I have my tea, I feel relaxed and peaceful from inside. If you haven't tried drinking your tea with mindfulness you should give it a try. You may just find it to be a good way to bring yourself back to the present moment, and prepare yourself for the day.

# Meditate

We don't know so many things about our life.

We don't know why we feel pain, or why we suffer, or why we fail to live a happy life, even when we don't do anything wrong. When we go through a crisis, we ask ourself why did it happen to us, and not to anyone else.

We have so many questions about ourself, to which we want the answers, but don't know how.

We try one solution after another, but never seem to find the right answers that fully satisfy us.

I have struggled with all such issues in past, and I still struggle with them every day. And every time, the only thing that helps me to find the right answers is Meditation.

Meditation helps you solve every problem of your life, if you allow it to do so. When you stop to look for answers outside, and start to look for them within you, you'll always find them, no matter how hard your problems are.

And the answers you find through meditation are always the one that are in perfect sync with your inner self. You will know when you find the perfect solution to your problems, that are unique to you.

Meditation helps you understand the nature of your body and mind. It helps you to understand yourself at such deep levels, that even the best psychologists can't match. It helps you to find even those answers which you can't find in books.

Meditation helps you become independent, and learn from the self.

It helps you find permanent solutions to your life problems, and not quick-fixes as most other methods do. It gives you the reasons for your actions, and makes you understand why you do what you do.

Meditation also helps you to do all your duties without attachment. It helps you to do what's important and necessary, and let go what's not.

We like to control every moment of our life, and when things don't happen as per our way, we feel unhappy and angry. Meditation helps you to gain control over yourself, and yet be happy and peaceful when things go wrong.

So, whenever you feel unhappy, confused, or clueless about your life, don't search for the solution outside in books, teachers, or on the internet. Instead, sit down, close your eyes, relax, focus on your breathe, and meditate on the problem. And you'll find the solution soon.

How soon the solutions come to you depends upon the nature of your problems and the depth of your meditation. While simple problems may take few minutes, some deeper problems may take you days, months, or even years to solve.

But, whatever your problem, meditation will help you find the best solution, which will also be a permanent one, to your problems.

Start practicing it today whenever you get time and at whatever place you can. You don't need a sound-proof house, or a deep forest to meditate. If you really want to meditate, you'll find several opportunities to do so, in your regular life. You can practice it while waiting in a queue, on your way home in a bus, or at your desk.

The practice of meditation will open new doors for you. You'll find you are becoming more happy and peaceful with each day. You'll find that, suddenly, you seem to know what's the right thing to do in any situation. You'll find all these and much more as you keep meditating every day.

I hope this article makes you start your meditation practice from today, if you haven't already done so.

Start meditating and the answers will soon start coming.

# Listen to Your Inner Self

Do you ever spend any time listening to your inner self?

You listen to your friends. You listen to your family. You listen to your teachers.

And you listen to your mind and your heart, too. Right?

But when I refer to listening to your inner self, I don't mean any of the above.

To listen to your inner self, go beyond your body, go beyond your mind, and go beyond your heart. There is something inside you that's separate from all these; listen to that.

If you want to learn more about your true nature, you need to form the habit of listening to your inner self daily.

By listening to the inner self you understand everything you want to know about yourself – you understand your thoughts, you understand your desires, you understand your feelings, you understand all the sensations going inside your body.

And that's just the first step towards understanding

yourself.

The second step is to go beyond them and dive deep down into yourself. That's where you'll discover things about yourself that you didn't even know exists. This state is nothing but the absence of everything you know. It's a state of total silence and peace.

In this state there is no mind, no heart, no body. That means there is also no thoughts, no desires, no feelings. It's a state you'll wish you can stay in forever.

But the question of staying in this state comes later.

First, the important thing is to discover it, and that's where many of us fail. Sometimes we give up easily, and other times we don't even try to listen to this inner self as we let other unwanted things run our life.

But if you ignore your inner self you'll never find permanent peace and happiness in your life. Your inner self is the reason you exist, and is it asking too much of yourself to give some time to listen to it?

Once you start listening to your inner self, you won't need any guru or teacher to tell you what to do. You will be able to make decisions as good as anyone else in your position.

Your inner self can guide you in situations even when your mind and heart fail to.

Now you may ask how can you listen to this inner self?

The tool that'll help you to listen to your inner self is meditation; it will help you find the "real" you.

By meditating every day, you bring yourself more and more closer to your inner self. This inner self is nothing but your consciousness that is always there inside you. The only reason you can't find it easily is because you have let other things dominate it for a long time.

Meditation helps you get rid of the unimportant things so that you can focus all your energy on the important ones; in this case, your inner self.

So, starting today, now is even better, spend some time every day to listen to your inner self. If you are willing to listen to it, you'll automatically find the energy and the time to do so.

As it takes time to discover your inner self, the more you delay to search for it, the harder it becomes. Start today, and you'll come closer to discovering your inner self by a day.

# Live Inside Out

How often do you find yourself do something, even when you know it's the wrong thing to do.

Quite regularly, right?

You get angry, or act selfishly, and then you wish you hadn't done so. Or sometimes, you let others disturb your inner peace, and you act impulsively, only to regret it later.

This happens to all of us.

I meditate every day, and try to remain calm all the time, yet I find myself losing control several times in a day; even over trivial things.

And it's during these times that I've to remind myself to stay calm and listen closely to my thoughts and feelings, and then take only that action which I know deep down inside me to be the right one.

I know you, too, come across several situations in your day-to-day life that tempt you to do the wrong thing.

And many times, you do end up doing the wrong thing even when you know the right thing to do.

Do you know why this happens?

This happens because you are used to living from the outside in, i.e. letting outer events affect and manipulate your inner well-being. And as long as you let yourself live based on outer conditions, you'll never be able to live a happy life.

When your happiness depends upon other people, or outside conditions, you are bound to feel unhappy for the simple reason: it's impossible for you to control the outside world.

If you try to control anything, besides yourself, you'll get frustrated and unhappy.

If you want to change that, it's time you started living from the inside out.

So let's see what it means to live from the inside out.

Put simply, it means to live your life in such a way that you are true to yourself every moment of your life. It means to do things that you know deep down to be the right thing to do, and not letting any outside event change it.

For example, suppose a friend or relative says something that hurts you. You become instantly angry and defend yourself or insult them in return.

You know anger is not good for you. Yet you let your anger dominate your mind and body. And you let that happen to you just because something happened, over which you had no control.

So, let's see how we can deal with the same situation when we live from the inside out.

Now, as the person says the words that hurt you, you can see the anger arising inside you. As it arises, you simply observe it without getting involved with it. You think of yourself not as a participant, but as a witness to the event. And then once you have recognized the event for what it is, you can let the anger dissolve inside you, and respond calmly.

So, you see, even for the same situation there can be two different outcomes: you can let the situation win over your inner self, or you can let your inner self win over the situation. Which one will you prefer?

The answer is obvious – you'll choose the one that is best for the well-being of your body and mind.

When you live from the inside out, you are in perfect control of your thoughts, feelings, and actions. No amount of outer chaos can affect the inner peace in you.

Instead of being carried away like a twig, and letting the wind take you wherever it wants, you can be the solid rock that remains steady even when the wind is at its strongest.

The outer world is uncontrollable, but you can control your inner world. While you can't control the events in your life that happen to you, you can surely control how you respond to those events.

When you live from the inside out, then everything you do is an action that you intend to do, and not a reaction that automatically happens by you.

We are meant to live from the inside out, but thanks to our conditioning by our society and culture we learn to live from the outside in. And then we wonder why we feel unhappy and stressed out all the time.

So for today, just try to live from the inside out and see how far you can do it without letting the outer world affect you. Then try it again tomorrow, and check if you did any better. Keep repeating this until you start living from the inside out naturally, without any effort, just as nature intended you to live.

# Empty Out

When you begin to learn meditation, it's a good idea to start with an empty mind.

Here's why.

As each day passes, you learn something new in your life. Every day your brain gets new ideas and experiences, which it promptly remembers so that it can use them later.

But what happens over a period of time, as months and years pass by, is that your mind gets completely filled with these past thoughts and actions. And when this happens, it becomes difficult to learn new ways of thinking and experiencing.

And your past knowledge and experience thus becomes a stumbling block in your meditation practice.

To learn and grow in meditation, you have to form new ways of thinking and observing this world. But if you cling to your past beliefs and actions, it becomes difficult to form new experiences that meditation has in store for you.

If you sit down to meditate, you'll find plenty of thoughts in your mind based on your old beliefs, knowledge, culture, and experience, that block you from going deep into meditation.

There is only one way you can deal with these unwanted thoughts in your mind, and that is to let them go.

Just like a filled cup only overflows, when you try to fill it further, the same way our mind too spills over any new thoughts, if it's already filled with other thoughts.

So the first step to cleanse your mind, and prepare it for meditation, is to empty out your mind, and let go everything that holds you back from giving hundred percent to your meditation practice.

When you let go everything, your mind automatically becomes peaceful. This is the state of emptiness. Before you do anything else, and fill your mind again with new thoughts, first, spend some time in this emptiness.

Live in this emptiness. Enjoy this emptiness. Stay as long as you can in this emptiness.

In this emptiness, you can see how insignificant everything around you is, and how temporary all the things in this world are.

The more you empty out, the more capacity you'll have to gain new knowledge. When you let go the unwanted thoughts that you clung to before, you are ready to let new wisdom and new understanding get inside you.

Empty out and then your mind will be ready to learn new things, and it will eagerly feed and nourish upon what you feed it now.

To learn meditation, is to make your mind empty again and again, and then fill it again and again with newer and deeper thoughts, that advance you further in understanding your inner self.

So, let your mind be empty once again, just like it was empty when you were born. But this time, instead of letting the world fill your mind with what the world wants you to be, fill it yourself with what you want yourself to be.

And your daily practice of meditation will help you fill your mind with the right thoughts that you need to live a happy and meaningful life.

# Live from Moment to Moment

Life is meant to be lived one moment at a time.

But we are always in such hurry that we fail to live our life in the present moment.

We are worried about our past. We are worried about our future. Throughout the day, we think about everything except the present moment.

A meaningful life isn't to live in future or past. It's to live in moment to moment.

When you learn to live your life from moment to moment, you become more mindful, and start to understand the reality and the power of the present moment.

When you live in the present moment, you don't judge or compare things, as there is nothing to be compared.

In the present moment, there is no past and no future, so what will you compare the present moment to?

Your only awareness is on the moment right in front of you, and you are totally absorbed living in it.

As one moment passes, you leave it and move on to the next moment.

You don't get attached with the previous moment. You don't look forward to the next moment.

You accept a moment as it is.

To live in the moment, act like an observer, and not as a participant.

Simply witness the present moment without judging it and without any desire to make it stay.

This act of observing the moment without any attachment is the first step towards living with mindfulness.

Now let's try to understand the nature of a single moment with an example.

Take a look at the waves in a sea. Look how the waves move. Each wave rises, stays for a while, and then falls down. Then another wave rises, stays, and falls down.

This goes on and on and on.

Each wave lives only for a moment. In reality the wave is nothing but just water all the time. It's we who give it an identity. When air pushes water, a wave is formed. When a wave falls down, it mixes with the water and loses its identity.

To understand the nature of water is to understand the nature of wave itself.

The same way, take a look at the thoughts in your mind. Observe how thoughts flow in your mind. Each thought comes, stays, and then goes away from your mind. Then another thought comes, stays, and goes away.

This goes on and on and on.

Each thought lives only for a moment. In reality a thought is nothing but just a temporary creation of mind. It's we who give it an identity. When desire pushes our mind, a thought is formed. When a thought ends, it dissolves in our mind and loses its identity.

To understand the nature of mind is to understand the nature of thought itself.

Just like the waves in a sea and the thoughts in our mind, the moments in our life too don't have any real existence.

In our life, a moment comes, stays, and then goes away. It's we who give it a name, an identity.

Once a moment ends, it loses its identity. Yet we burden our minds with it.

And if that's not enough, we burden ourself with thoughts and events that haven't even happened yet.

To live a meaningful life, you've to learn to let go the past and the future, and live your life from moment to moment.

Understand this simple way of living, and you'll understand life itself.

# Live with Consciousness

So far in this book, we have covered a lot of things that are essential to live a meaningful life.

We started with simplifying our life, then we saw how to overcome our negative qualities, and then we learned about the nature of our mind and how to live in the present moment.

Now we come to the final chapter of this book, which talks about living with consciousness.

Once you learn to live with consciousness all your worries in life fade away, and you start to live your life with purpose.

Consciousness is also known by several other names such as your presence or your inner self. For this chapter, we'll stick with the word consciousness.

To live with consciousness, first you've to understand what consciousness is.

Consciousness is that part of you that is timeless, and separate from your body and mind. It's separate from your ego, and your thoughts and feelings. It's something that cannot be defined in terms of a single word.

It's difficult to explain consciousness to someone who doesn't know anything about it, and it's difficult to understand it if you don't keep an open mind and take efforts to know it.

You either realize it and start learning more about it, or you think it's completely nonsense and ignore anyone who talks about it. Not many people want to talk about it, but I think it's essential to understand it to live a meaningful life.

Many people live their whole life, even without once realizing the nature of their consciousness. It's that difficult to understand; not by it's nature, but because of our narrowly conditioned mind.

You don't have to go anywhere to realize your consciousness. It's always present in you; you just have to take the right effort to understand it.

Till you realize it, your consciousness remains quietly inside you. Once recognized, you become aware of something in you, that's separate from your mind, and yet capable enough to make the right decisions for you; decisions that consider the well-being of every life form in this planet, and which I dare say are as per the rules of this universe.

And these decisions come from a deeper understanding, not the superficial understandings of the mind. When you are fully conscious, you'll even know when to use your mind, and when to not.

I'll be lying if I say I live in this state all the time, or if I've completely understood it. But it's something I've been trying to understand for several years now.

What I can tell though is that it's a place where even your mind can't reach. It's the thing you feel inside you when you read spiritual books or listen to spiritual talks. It's the thing you become aware of in your deeper states of meditation.

Unfortunately, instead of consciousness, the main focus of the civilized world is the mind. You let your mind run your life and make every decision for you. You rely on your mind too much, and this causes you happiness and sorrow, from time to time.

When you let your mind make all your decisions, then things that work according to it give you happiness, and things that don't work according to it give you sorrow.

What you need to do is to move beyond this circle of happiness and sorrow, and discover your true purpose in life. For that, you need to break the boundaries of your mind, and go beyond it towards something that's far greater – your consciousness.

Now you may want to know if it's possible for every one to understand how to live with consciousness? And if yes, then how?

Yes, it's possible for anyone to realize this conscious state. Consciousness isn't a skill that only a few can master; it doesn't rely upon talent that only a few can have. You have as much ability to realize it as I have, or as anyone else has.

To understand consciousness, first, you have to remove all the barriers that come between you and your consciousness. The biggest barriers are your desires, your thoughts, your feelings, your ego i.e. your sense of I'ness, and your own mind.

Practicing meditation and mindfulness every day can help you to overcome all these barriers one by one. Often it takes several years of practice to remove these barriers fully from within you. But you instantly feel deep peace from within, whenever you remove any of these barriers completely.

The more barriers you remove, the more peaceful and meaningful your life becomes.

If all this seems too difficult to understand, don't worry. With time you will understand everything.

There is so much to know about consciousness, that if you try to force yourself to understand it in few minutes, you'll only get more and more confused.

So for now, I just want you to practice mindfulness and meditation every day, for as much time as you possibly can. Practice this for a few weeks, and you will start to see positive changes in your life. And one day you will surely learn to live in sync with your consciousness.

Once you start to see things consciously and act accordingly, you'll see how simple and beautiful life already is. You will feel a deep sense of completeness from within, and you will want nothing else from life.

And that's when you will start to live each day of your life for a greater purpose, and your actions will spread happiness and peace across this world.

Now, as we come to the end of this book and before you close it, I want you to close your eyes for a few minutes, and think upon what you have learned till now. More than what you've read, I want you to apply all this knowledge you have gained, in your day-to-day life.

Practice living with simplicity every day. Practice living with mindfulness every day. Practice meditation every day. And with each day, your life will become more and more meaningful.

I wish you all the best.

The ~~End~~ Beginning...

# About the Author

Rahul Singh is an Indian author and writer. He writes regularly on his blog Life Beginner, where he helps others find inner peace, lasting happiness, and meaning in their lives, by showing them the way of mindfulness, meditation, and simple living. To read more from him and to get his latest writings directly in your email inbox, you can visit his site at www.lifebeginner.com and signup for free email updates.

CPSIA information can be obtained
at www.ICGtesting.com
Printed in the USA
LVHW082125171220
674456LV00029B/640